AF255713

Knowing and Being
Breema and the Meaning of Your Life

Also from The Breema Center

BOOKS:

Coming to Yourself: *The Art of Practicing Breema*

Your Home Is the Entire Cosmos: *The Wisdom of Breema*

Real Health Means Harmony with Existence:
The Art of Practicing Breema

First You Have to Be:
The Nine Principles of Harmony in Breema and Life

The Taste of Being Present: *Essential Wisdom of Breema*

Child of Existence, Child of Society

Breema and the Nine Principles of Harmony

Waking Up to This Moment: *The Essential Meaning of Breema*

The Four Relationships and Other Essential Insights

In the Garden of All Possibilities: *Essential Poetry*

In the Heart of the Moment: *Essential Poetry*

Freedom Is in This Moment: *365 Insights for Daily Life*

Every Moment Is Eternal: *The Timeless Wisdom of Breema*

Freedom Comes from Understanding: *Insights for Meaningful Life*

Seeing Things As They Really Are

AUDIO CDs:

Please see our website and the back pages of this book for audio
CDs of Breema Center books.

eBOOKS:

Download Breema eBooks from your favorite online book source.

TRANSLATIONS:

Despertando a este momento: *el significado esencial de Breema*

Selbst-Breema: *Übungen für ein harmonisches Leben*

Breema und die neun Prinzipien der Harmonie

Knowing and Being

*Breema and the
Meaning of Your Life*

by Jon Schreiber

The Breema Center
Oakland, California

The Breema Center
6076 Claremont Avenue
Oakland, CA 94618

phone: 510.428.0937
email: center@breema.com
website: breema.com

Knowing and Being: *Breema and the Meaning of Your Life*

Library of Congress Control Number: 2021915812
Printed in USA

Print ISBN: 978-1-7336310-3-7
eBook ISBN: 978-1-7336310-4-4

Front jacket photograph by jakkapan, used under license from Shutterstock
Back jacket photograph by WPixz, used under license from Shutterstock

Breema®, Self-Breema® — Breema and Self-Breema are service marks of the Breema Center.

Your actual responsibility in life is the evolution of your consciousness. This doesn't take place by itself. You have to discover that wish in yourself— the desire to understand who you are, to understand the meaning and purpose of your life. You initiate yourself into the reality of Existence. No one can do that for you.

Contents

Introduction

The purpose of Breema is to help us move out of the unconscious state, by raising our level of consciousness. In other words, Breema is here to help you fulfill your purpose as a human being.

In truth, there is nothing more rewarding than stepping onto this road and walking. Breema tells us that we need to develop ourselves, and shows us how to see and experience this essential need for ourselves. It points us in the direction we wish to go, and supplies us with the practical knowledge we need to correctly use the tools that were given to us to enable us to develop. Every step we take, even the smallest, comes with a deep satisfaction, as we begin to discover that the Nine Principles of Harmony indicate the natural state of our mind, feelings, and body as we move towards greater harmony within ourselves and with the entire universe.

After more than forty years studying, practicing, and teaching Breema bodywork, Self-Breema exercises, and Breema's philosophy of living, my appreciation and gratitude for Breema only grows stronger.

Working with Breema's most elementary guidance—"Bring your mind to your body"—we find a foundation that affords us entry into the *existing* universe of reality, meaning, and purpose. Here, we find real freedom and our true home. We can begin to fulfill our natural potential to be in harmony with everyone and everything that exists.

I hope that these simple writings, which come from classes taught at the Breema Center, will reveal their meaning to you, again and again, each time in a new and deeper way, as they continue to do for me.

— Jon Schreiber

Knowing and Being
Breema and the
Meaning of Your Life

BREEMA
The Nine Principles of Harmony

BODY COMFORTABLE

When we look at the body, not as something separate,
but as an aspect of a unified whole,
there is no place for discomfort.

NO EXTRA

To express our True nature, nothing extra is needed.

FIRMNESS AND GENTLENESS

Real firmness is always gentle.
Real gentleness is always firm.
When we are present, we naturally
manifest firmness and gentleness simultaneously.

FULL PARTICIPATION

The most natural way of moving and living is with
full participation. Full participation is possible when
body, mind, and feelings are united in a common aim.

MUTUAL SUPPORT

*The more our Being participates, the more we are able to
support life and recognize that Existence supports us.
Giving and receiving support take place simultaneously.*

NO JUDGMENT

*The atmosphere of nonjudgment gives us a taste of
acceptance of ourselves as we are in the moment. When
we come to the present, we are free from judgment.*

SINGLE MOMENT/SINGLE ACTIVITY

*Each moment is new, fresh, totally alive. Each moment
is an expression of our True nature, complete by itself.*

NO HURRY/NO PAUSE

*In the natural rhythm of life energy,
there is no hurry and no pause.*

NO FORCE

*When we let go of assumptions of separation,
we let go of force.*

Always and everywhere, there is the possibility to wake up. There is something in us that is free from time, yet includes all time. It is free from space, yet all space is within it. It is free from words, yet all words announce it. It is free from shape, texture, and color, free from mind, feelings, sensations, free from "here" and "there," yet gives reality to all of those.

It is so timeless, it appears as time. It's so present in time, it becomes timeless. It is nameless, but all names come from it. It is unborn, yet a part of it is in everything that appears. It's the relationship between lover and beloved, yet is free of both.

It is love itself, self-created and existing beyond time and space, beyond the manifested universe, yet its attributes could be received from all that exists.

It is neither real nor unreal. It's where the question of real and unreal doesn't arise. In its presence, everything finds refuge in peace and rest, yet it is always awake.

You cannot find it by searching, because in every stage of your search, you are moving away from it. If you reach for it, you have gone too far.

It is you, yourself, without the words "you" or "yourself." It is the silence beyond vibrations, and it's the manifestation of vibration. It is matter, it is energy, it is Consciousness, it is Awareness, and yet, it is not. The dance of the cosmos expresses its beauty and its magnitude, yet it is free from movement.

Its thought becomes Law. The Law manifests and the universe appears, yet it is free from appearance. You cannot see it, but you see everything with it. You cannot touch it, but all that you touch, you touch with it. You cannot think it, but thought is its manifestation.

Nothing exists without it. Nothing exists with it, because it alone has existence.

Every step towards it brings inner satisfaction. Every step away from it creates suffering. The diversified universe is its expression, and unity is the nature of its being. It resides in the heart and illuminates the mind. It is expressed through your eyes and is received through impression.

You cannot find it, because it's never been lost. You cannot be it as long as you take yourself to be separate from it. It gives freedom to make choices, and guidance in how to choose.

It exists in all dimensions, and the relationship between all dimensions creates the pageant of life. It gives meaning to the meaningless, and wisdom to ignorance. It gives joy to the sorrowful heart. It's the beauty in the beautiful. It's clarity in the movement of thoughts and feelings. It's hidden from the eyes of the wise, and is revealed to the innocent. It is *is-ness* itself, and contains all that exists within itself. It looks at the manifested universe, but sees only itself. Its benevolent quality gives us the possibility to know it. It's hidden and it's obvious, and it is also the relationship between hidden and obvious.

All moments of life are blessings, if we are present. We have to clearly see that the past is gone and the future is "elsewhere." But in this moment, we could be here, present. If there's something you need to do to repair the past, you still have to do it in this moment. In the present, there's always a chance to take a correct step for your life. If you need to prepare for the future, you can only do it in the present. That's where all your possibilities are.

We are filled with worry, anxiety, fear, and everything that comes with them. We don't understand the meaning of being present. Only in a moment that we're present do we know. We don't have command over our mind, our feelings, and not even over our own body. To think "I'm in charge" is an illusion. But we have the possibility to see our condition, and then to see what steps we can take to free ourselves from this slavery to our fragmented and undisciplined mind, body, and feelings.

To start, we need to see that our mind, feelings, and body don't work together. They don't have a common aim. Each is in its own world. Our mind and feelings are usually in conflict, and they don't understand what the body actually is and how to be with it. We see our body's reflection in the mirror, and we hear people call our name when they see this body, but we don't enter into its existence, its meaning. We don't even really know how to take care of it. We don't know how to free it from tension and inertia. Our feelings are slaves to what we like and dislike. Our mind is always in a state—daydreaming and imagining, or filled with useless, uninvited thoughts which chatter with each other as our life passes by mechanically. The sooner we see and accept that this is our condition, the sooner we can take a step in the direction of finding something in ourselves that can be in charge of our mind, feelings, and body.

To live fully, we need something that's entirely missing in our lives—a real *I*. Ordinarily, when we say "I," we don't really know who or what we're referring to, because a real *I* is missing. Our thoughts, feelings, and sense organs function with mechanical energy. They don't have light to see with. That's why we don't see our own thoughts and feelings. And we rarely know we have a body. But the real *I* functions with Conscious energy. Consciousness has light, and with it, we can see how to go through life and fulfill our purpose for being on this Earth—we can have a meaningful life.

To live fully means having this Conscious *I* participating in our life. Only then can we say we're fully living. And that doesn't just happen by itself. Strong desire and a lot of preparation are needed. We need to see through the purposeless life we live day after day. We have to see there is the possibility of living consciously. We need to taste this Conscious *I* in order to find our direction.

Body-mind connection is our entry. When we accustom the mind to remain with the body—to stay with the process of inhalation and exhalation, for example—we create room in ourselves. Instead of being totally filled with useless thoughts, there is room to invite Conscious energy. With its light, we can see our direction.

The self we know is not our true self. The world we know is not the real world, because our "knowing" is in a dimension ruled by thought, and thought is always far from reality. So the thing to do is to find something simple you can do to *taste* you are present. Real knowing is in taste. Your body is always manifesting, always doing something. It's always breathing. Bring the attention of your mind to that. When the mind's attention is completely with your body's manifestation, you have body-mind connection. Body-mind connection connects you to your essential self.

You can't tell your mind "Don't think." That's its job. You can't tell your feelings "Don't feel." You can't put your mind and feelings out of work even if you want to. They're not going to give up their jobs! Your mind has to think, and your feelings have to feel. The problem is that when we think and feel, we go to the past and future, and we're not present.

When you come out of your mind, where do you come to? You come to life. Life is in this present moment. And there's something that lets you know you're present in life—you taste *there is a body*.

Mass consciousness is always affecting us, keeping us in a hypnotic state. We don't really know who we are. We just assume things, and go through life that way. We don't enter into the meaning of life.

Because we don't have real consciousness, we're not conscious of our existence. We need that consciousness. With it, you can bring the attributes of your Timeless nature to your everyday life. With it, you can manifest with the light, wisdom, and compassion of your highest nature. When you know *there is a body*, you minimize the influence of mass consciousness on you. It's as though the "you" you think you are disappears. The only thing that remains is knowing *Existence exists*.

When you are connected to your body, you are connected to all life. You are connected to the entire Existence. Thought isn't needed. In fact, nothing is needed. Without thoughts, feelings, or sensations, you have a taste of being "in." You belong to the entire universe, and nothing is separated. The sense and taste of unity is also the sense and taste of your own existence. You could say "I exist," or "Everything exists." In the realizable universe, you realize the entirety.

To be present means to not be in the past or the future. But it's very difficult to not be in the past or future. Why? Simply because we are creatures who think, and thoughts are always in the past or future. And we live in the world of our senses, which, by nature, are comparative. Something seems soft compared to something that seems hard. Something seems warm compared to something that seems cold. Because we compare, we go to our memories to interpret the language of our senses. To be present, we need a new way to work with our senses, our thoughts, and our feelings.

If you allow your senses to receive sensory impressions, and ask your mind and feelings not to interpret them, your consciousness receives a *direct* impression of what is. Your relationship to your life and to the world of phenomena becomes a *direct* relationship. In a *direct* relationship, judgment drops. You take an impression of Existence, and see things as they are.

There's no need to try to hold on to a moment of Consciousness. Instead, see what "extra" you're holding on to; see what's obscuring reality. That's a worthwhile direction—to let go of extra.

Everything comes from the Source. If we take that as the whole truth, and ignore the dynamic nature of the universe, we miss the meaning. That which comes from the Source also needs to return to the Source. Awareness emanates and creates Consciousness. But the universe also includes energy and matter. We can't understand the universe unless we look at the purpose.

It's said that a drop of water becomes heavier until it reaches the bottom of the ocean. Then it needs to come back to the surface.

What is your actual position in the universe in this very moment? Part of it is your relationship to the world of time and space, the world of events, and part is your relationship to the eternal aspect, to the realizable universe.

When you *realize*, you *are*. That actually means you are on the tightrope between the observable and realizable. Your job is to remain on the tightrope—to remain *awake*. The tightrope is the line of awakening. Each moment of awakening has one purpose—to support you to wake up again to a higher dimension of consciousness. This is the eternal process, beginningless and endless.

What happens in this process? Conscious energy is created. When this inner light shines, you can see the entire process of Existence.

With the light of Consciousness, you see "outside" and "inside" simultaneously. You see Existence, *and* yourself as an included part of it. The reality of yourself is the process of *seeing*. By seeing, you come to Being, and from Being, you come to understanding. The reality of you is your understanding. In a moment of understanding, you are awake. At the moment of death, you lose your body, your mind, your feelings, and your sensory perceptions. But not your understanding! Understanding is eternal.

Your fear (and everything of that nature) only seems to exist—where there's an absence of light. It's there because *you* are not. There is a seat inside of you. And only one person can sit on it. Everyone you've put on that seat, or allowed to sit there, is imaginary. But you believe in them. So the real you doesn't have a place to sit. You have to get the others out of the chair, so it becomes available for the real you to sit in it. How? Come to the body. Breathe. Come to your weight. Do that, and then, it's no longer occupied by others.

We don't exist the way we think of ourselves (as something separate, independent of the rest of Existence). That's imaginary. We exist only because Existence exists. Reality has to be there. That makes us real. If reality disappears, we disappear too. But if we disappear, reality is still there!

If you come to the body, and make that seat available, and then come to a tiny taste of reality, you find a thread of connection to yourself. Reality is always there, just like the sky. You only have to stop looking away from it! When you lose connection to reality, it simply means you are looking at imaginary things. The reality of yourself is timelessly present in time. Your life originated from that which you are in reality, from Existence itself.

One of our chief difficulties is that we believe we are this body. Even if you say "No, that's not what I think," that "no" is theoretical, because we don't know anything else. We are so identified with our name and body, with what we see when we look in the mirror.

But when you look in the mirror, it's not actually you who is looking. Your eyes look, but you translate that into how you imagine others may see you. We don't have a drop of our own consciousness. Instead, mass consciousness is operating in us, and we all think that's us. And on top of that, the "you" you think you are is constantly replaced by another "you." You have a thousand different "I's," each of which is in charge of you for a short time. Each of those "I's" calls itself by your name. So you think you are one person.

Why don't we ask ourselves, "Why am I not as I truly wish to be?" Every one of us knows something is not as it should be. This machinery we call "me" is going to die. Can we prevent that? No. Yet we decide to not think of it. If you knew for sure that you would die on a certain date in the near future, would you live your life the way you do? Would your values be what they are now?

True health means health in the body, health in the emotions, in the mind, and in spirit. Spirit is that which *exists*. It's that which is present. It's that which is connected to the Source. It sees in both directions—"above" and "below" itself. What it manifests is Consciousness.

When you wake up to your connection with the Ultimate Source, the eternal passes through the temporary, and you come to the Moment. Your real *I* is present, and becomes *I am*. When you have that *I*, you are actually healthy. When you are actually healthy, you develop. To develop means to fulfill your potential.

It's said we are created in the image of God. But that has to become reality, through self-development. The seed of Consciousness that has been given to us needs to sprout.

We are self-developing. No one else can make you develop. You have to become yourself in reality. All the true Teachings that have ever been on this Earth have given guidance on how to develop ourselves. But we have to participate in our own completion. For that, we need self-familiarity, self-knowledge, self-understanding, and finally, self-transformation. In self-transformation, we enter and become one with the Source of our existence.

I is the Ultimate within you. *Am* is the expression of that *I*.

You receive energy from above, from "heaven," and you bring it to your "earth." "Heaven" is what you understand. "Earth" is the aspect of you that hasn't received understanding yet. It needs to receive light.

We study things to try to make them "concrete" and exact. But in doing so, we actually make them vague, conceptual, and static, instead of living and dynamic. So we see them as they are *not*, rather than as they actually are.

Just because we've memorized something, we think we understand it. But when we talk about it, it remains something from outside, something separate from us. We're not present in it. So it's not real knowledge.

Breema depends on one thing—knowing *there is a body* by *taste*. Your mind says "there is a body," but doesn't taste it. Your mind doesn't actually know your body is breathing. But if you ask the mind to register inhalation and exhalation, and continue registering long enough, it becomes quiet. It's as though the door of the mind opens, and the light of Consciousness shines in. Instead of thoughts, we have *realizations*.

When you taste *I have a body* enough, you begin to understand that you are not this body. You may even begin to see that the body is in you, not vice versa! And that the body is made of the same thing you're made of—Consciousness.

We have nothing. You don't own your mind. You don't own your feelings. You don't own your body. They own you! When you get angry, your anger owns you—it's your master. Your thoughts own you and become your master, because you're not really present, you're not home.

There is something that could be yours—your Being-existence. But you have to work for it. The first step is to see you're not present. When you see you're not present, that gives you the possibility to actually be here. Bring your mind and body together. That's the key. And stay with that—keep bringing them together. That you can do.

We think literally. In literal thinking, we look at things as opposites. For example, we think clarity and confusion are opposites. Yet we have the possibility to think relatively. In relative thinking, we see they are not opposites. They are simply two different dimensions of consciousness.

Looking at things as opposites breeds violence. So the disadvantage of literal thinking is huge.

Relative thinking can give us some insight. Thinking literally, you imagine you know who you are. But with relative thinking, you see that you don't really know.

When you look relatively, many dimensions become visible. You become increasingly insignificant, because as you look from each higher, more inclusive dimension, it's as though you "shrink," you become smaller. There are seven billion of us on this one planet, and planet Earth itself is like a speck of dust in the Milky Way. That's what happens when you look relatively—you find your true significance, by seeing your nothingness. In seeing that, you enter into the reality of yourself. You *are* and you are not. That's a magnificent thing for a person to discover.

The moments in which you have understanding are
your life. When you understand, you *exist*. If you have
two moments of existence in seventy years, those two
moments are your life, not all the time in between.

Everything that functions by using energy mechanically, unconsciously, is subject to deteriorate and eventually disappear. Look at humanity—look at the extent to which we have degenerated. We're like monsters—in our thoughts, in our feelings, and in our actions. We manipulate others in order to get what we think we want. And actually, that is exactly what we *don't* want. That's why we need to develop—to transform mechanical energy into Consciousness.

The whole universe is so simple when you actually *see* it. Then your feeling is: "Of course! It couldn't be any other way."

What we want brings us misery and suffering. If we go after what we want, we mechanically use energy. But what we need doesn't come only through mechanical energy. Take something simple, like food, for example. When you eat as much as you need, you feel good and you gain energy from it. But as soon as your need is fulfilled, if you continue eating, based on what you want, you feel sick, tired, and your energy is drained.

Existence is one whole unity, but it manifests in everything distinctively, particularly. That's why everything matters. That's why self-development is needed. No one can develop you—you have to do it. Understanding is not general—it has to be particular. You can't do exactly the same thing anyone else does—it wouldn't work for you. Someone else cannot know, for example, how much you should eat—only you can know.

The events of life flow and affect each of us differently. They're telling you something, telling you that you have to be present in order to deal with them. Nothing else will work. We are not meant to to go through life in sleep. We need to wake up!

Our life on this Earth is not an accidental phenomenon. We are meant to be here, and we have a "destiny" to fulfill. It may be hard for us to understand this, but our destiny is not something unchangeable. If we are able to come to a higher level of consciousness, our level of Being changes. Each level of Being is subject to different Universal Laws and influences. When you understand that, you can see that you are not bound by what you were before. Each moment of your life is a new opportunity to manifest, not mechanically or by habit, but according to your understanding. You may see that you are not your past, because it's possible to be free from your past. You can also be free from your future, as strange as that may sound. By increasing your consciousness, you could have a life rooted in this moment, which arises from awareness of your existence, a life in which you can manifest your understanding.

Knowledge doesn't necessarily lead to understanding. You could have tremendous knowledge but no understanding. Our problem is that we don't see the difference between knowledge that's just in our head, and knowledge that becomes part of our Being—knowledge that's been experienced and understood, and then manifested as understanding.

You can accept things as they are only if you accept yourself as you are. First, you have to know this "you" you want to accept. Why is "Who am I?" not our question? If you really wish to know, it means you've seen that you don't know. And to accept that you don't know is the hardest thing in the world! Because from day one, we've received praise and admiration for showing that we know something. But underneath it, there is an ocean of ignorance. So we don't allow ourselves to see ourselves as we are. Instead, we take our thoughts about ourselves, our images, and our ideas, to be us.

To accept things as they are, you have to accept yourself as you are. To do that, you have to have knowledge about this "you" you want to accept. But that knowledge is not enough. Knowledge doesn't give you acceptance. As soon as you see what you are, you also find you don't want to be that. And what you wish to be, you cannot be, unless you have understanding. So self-knowledge has to become self-understanding. The purpose of understanding yourself is to transform yourself—to come back to your True nature, to unite with the Source. Then you have *awareness* of your existence, which is also awareness of everything that exists. You and your True nature become one. You can accept things as they are according to the degree you understand yourself. In understanding, everything can be accepted.

If you look, you'll see that all the things you've done that you are sorry for, you did because you didn't have understanding. When you have understanding, the way you manifest is constructive and supports life.

Progress is made in time, but development takes place in the Moment.

We can divide humanity into three categories. The first, which includes nearly all of us, all seven billion people on this Earth, is the mechanical circle of humanity. That means we are motivated from outside, and we do everything mechanically; we don't actually experience where we are and what we do.

The second category is the balanced circle of humanity, those who strive in order to have mind, feelings, and body work together in unity towards Self-understanding.

The third category is the Conscious circle of humanity, those who have *awareness* of the fact that they exist. They are conscious, not only of themselves, but of all life that surrounds them.

With all the spiritual material available on the Earth, why is life still so chaotic? It's because we hear things associatively, and we either reject them or believe them based solely on our associations, without actually examining them. The first step has been left out. The first step is to make ourselves *able* to do right and not wrong. That ability has to be developed.

There is a possibility for us to become conscious human beings, because we have been given a seed of Consciousness. A conscious human being is someone who acts consciously with the support of Conscience to help bring things back towards harmony. People who have developed to higher levels of consciousness are needed, so the Universe can move towards greater harmony. The more we develop, the more we wish to support the Universal harmony.

To begin to move in that direction, we need to connect to our body. And we need to "empty" our crystallized mind and feelings by dis-identifying with everything they've unconsciously accumulated, so we can have new thoughts and new feelings, and a new posture towards life.

Our ordinary desires are acquired from outside. They are not really ours. They come from mass consciousness and create fear. To not be completely ruled by them, we need to connect to the body.

We need to keep our feet on the ground by coming to the body. Practice that whenever you can. Register body inhaling and exhaling, and stay with it until you are present in your body. This can give you more support than any philosophy! God is present when you are ready to experience God's presence. But we are not available when we're in the past or the future. When you come to your body, you become available to receive Conscious energy.

If you really see anything as it is, you see it in unity—you see the whole. If you look at matter and really see it, you see the Totality. You see that there is no separate matter. When you *see* form, you see the formless manifesting itself as form. That's why nothing is a fixed "thing." Because what appears in time is the manifestation of Timeless Existence. You are seeing the appearance in time of a timeless process.

A tree has roots which connect it to the earth, and via the earth, to the whole universe. Its trunk, branches, and leaves give it form. The relationship between its nature as the Totality and its relative nature as a form is expressed by the exchange taking place within the tree—the movement of its sap.

Everything, without exception, is included in Existence, as it is. Our identification with some aspect makes it separate in our imagination. That imaginary separation and the process of imagining—these, too, are included in Existence. For Existence, they are not a problem—they cannot be outside of the Totality, and there cannot be "someone" who is manifesting that way. There is only the Totality, so Existence is manifesting like that. At the moment we accept that we're identified, that we're imagining, then we *exist*. Even our imagination no longer separates us, because in truth, it can't and never did. We have an imaginary life and imaginary things. But the moment we connect to the presence of the real, everything becomes real, everything exists.

You cannot see that which is higher than your level of consciousness. When you try to, you only relate to a concept and identify with it. When we identify with any particular level, that identification becomes a conceptual wall and keeps us from seeing anything above that level. When you really *see*, you see the concept, and at the same time, see through it to the real nature of what you are looking at. You are in unity and whatever you are looking at, you see in unity. *Seeing* means seeing things as they are. You see Existence wherever you look.

Real understanding is understanding in freedom. That is the understanding that comes with *seeing*. You don't understand "something," because what you understand becomes "emptiness"—it disappears, yet exists within you. There is no "you" and no thing that you understand. There's just understanding, which exists in the Moment. You can't hold on to the form of what you've previously understood, because each form becomes a wall that encloses and limits you. Understanding in freedom means seeing through those walls, seeing that they also are made of light, so you and everything inside the structure they create are illuminated.

Nothing can be understood from a level of consciousness in which you only see the form, only the appearance of things. When you come to the Moment, you see things as they are. When you see that Existence *exists*, things appear as they do, and you can enjoy that. It gives color and spice to Existence, and at the same time, it's "transparent"—you can see that everything is pregnant with existence and is Existence.

49

Knowing *there is a body* is our entry into the unity of all that exists. It's the beginning of Consciousness. From there, we can come to taste *this body has life*, and then, to *life is eternal*.

The Universe is *one*, but we don't get anything by attaching ourselves to this statement, because we can't enter into it, we don't understand it. We first have to look at it as *two*, and from there enter into oneness, but in understanding. Seeing it as *two*, the dynamic of the Universe can be looked at and understood. There's not just matter—there's energy and matter. There's not just the Source—there's the Source and its manifestation. *One* becomes *two*, and *two* becomes many. From many, from the diversity of Existence, you have to come back again to *one*. This way, we can put things in perspective and increase our understanding.

The aim is Self-understanding. We need that in order to understand anything. We want to become conscious, we want to be initiated into higher dimensions of consciousness, but only self-initiation is possible. To come to the self we want to be conscious of, we have to distinguish between the unconscious and conscious dimensions. We have to see the false as false, and the real as real.

You are here to wake up. Whenever you see you are asleep, you should be happy! Because now you can wake up. Whatever you perceive with your senses is not something to get caught in. You see it in order to be reminded to wake up. Everything outside of you, everything that takes place outside of you, is there for you to use to become more essential, to move more inside. "The kingdom of God is within you." The meaning of everything outside, of all events, can be found in yourself.

If you *wake up*, you need to wake up again in the very next moment. When you think you are awake, it means you are asleep. When you're awake, there's no thought. Consciousness manifests without looking to see how it's manifesting. It doesn't need to try to describe or remember any characteristic of itself in order to try to manifest that way again.

When you are not awake, your sense organs are connected to your thoughts. What they take in elicits a reaction in you—in thoughts. But when you're awake, the senses receive an impression, and that impression is transformed in your consciousness. It becomes food for further awakening.

If you don't interpret what your senses take in, there is room for Consciousness to enter. Consciousness relates to things directly, not via definitions. With Consciousness, you can see things as they are. You can invite Consciousness to your life by bringing it to your body. Bring your mind to your breathing. That "empties" you enough to allow Consciousness to enter.

If several people are sitting together, only the person who *knows* he is sitting is supporting the others, because he *is* sitting.

To have self-acceptance, first, you need to see and understand the necessity for it. You need a strong desire for it.

If you don't accept yourself, you want to change yourself. But that's not at all easy! Even if you could, you don't know what aspect to change, and what to change it into. To change yourself in a way that's actually beneficial, you would need complete knowledge of yourself and of everything taking place around you. Once you see that you don't have that knowledge, you may be more ready to turn in the direction of acceptance. Start by accepting what you can, and just see that there are certain things you are not yet able to accept.

In true acceptance, there is understanding of yourself, and understanding of the purpose of Existence and your part in it. True acceptance is benevolent and belongs to a higher dimension of yourself.

To be yourself is a big thing! Ask yourself, "What do I want?" If you try to answer, you find that as soon as you mention one thing, you think of something else you also want. One lifetime isn't enough to get everything you want! Because we want a million things, we run around like a chicken without a head, and we constantly hurt each other. We don't behave the way we mean to. We say and do things without knowing why. That's why we have so many regrets. If we knew what we were doing, if we were connected to meaning and purpose, we wouldn't be afraid of the people we care about, nor would we hurt them. We wouldn't cause ourselves and others so many problems.

W hen you are truly present, everything falls into its proper place. You do the right things at the right time. Because you're in harmony, it's natural for you to do so.

We need to filter what comes to us. But instead, we indiscriminately take in everything, so we become filled up with garbage, with worthless information. We need to create a filtration system for ourselves by questioning and considering everything, by really looking into things. Then we have some choice, and can see where to invest our energy.

To use our mind in a meaningful way, we have to bring it to function in harmony with our body and feelings.

You can't know *directly* what the "life experience" of a salt-shaker is (assuming there is such a thing for a salt-shaker), because it cannot be your experience. If you look at the salt-shaker as matter and energy, you may be able to philosophize, but that knowledge wouldn't be direct. "Direct" means you receive that knowledge from your Being. It means there is a direct connection to your Being.

Everything you think about yourself is just a story about yourself. If someone asks, "Who are you?"—you go to thoughts, to the past. You say your name, your job, who your parents and grandparents were, who you like and don't like. You can go on forever without saying one word about yourself. You only talk about the stories that your body (which you think is you) has passed through. But where is the real you in that?

You are not an event. You are not your body. You are not your thoughts, feelings, or sensations. When you see that all those are only events, you see you are the Consciousness that is conscious of events.

Between who you think you are and who you really are, there is a valley. And that valley cannot be crossed by knowledge, information, by stories or hearsay. We have to differentiate between thought and Consciousness. No one can do that for you. You have to know it for yourself.

We think we are this body. If that were so, we would be born to die. But a universe of birth and death is a meaningless universe. If you look at Existence, you see it is too powerful to be meaningless. So we have to understand the body, this vehicle we've been given. The body is not only for relating to outer life. That's not its only purpose. It also needs to serve our inner life. Looking at the body this way, you have the possibility of understanding it. No matter how much you study anatomy and physiology, you cannot understand the body. You have to look at its purpose in relation to your inner life, too.

The body is an incredible phenomenon. Why does the Universe go through so much to create this instrument that lasts only seventy or eighty years? Because the body can receive every kind of energy that is in the Universe. Through it, we can know a particular type of energy that can help us wake up. What does it mean to wake up? It means to see who you are. Where do you come from? What's the purpose of coming to this Earth? To wake up means to enter into the meaning and purpose, to invite Conscious energy into your life.

Meaning and purpose cannot be understood through thoughts, feelings, or sensations. Only through Consciousness. What is Consciousness? Words cannot really tell you. Real things have to be *experienced*. They have to be *realized*. If it could be given in words, the whole planet would be conscious by now. But the possibility of experiencing it arises with your receptivity. Consciousness is emanated from your True nature, and it can penetrate and comprehend what it sees. The simplest way of saying it is that with Consciousness, you can see things as they are.

We can look at each other, but we don't see each other. Our eyes are like a camera—they take a picture. And immediately, we begin associating what they see with all kinds of other things. We don't really see each other. We see our images and associations—our thoughts about the "photos" our eyes take. We are afraid of each other because we just see the surface images. We don't see through to our essential nature. And whatever we don't understand, we're afraid of.

That's why Breema offers the Nine Universal Principles of Harmony. If you enter into these Principles, you have the possibility of understanding yourself, the Universe, and everything that exists.

A part that's conscious of its existence is also the entire Existence. All of creation comes from the same Source. The purpose of every relationship is to help lead you back to your Source.

What we identify so strongly with is just the movie of life, projected on a screen. If you see that this is so, you have a chance to lose the fear of seeing yourself as you are. You (the real you) are the one who sees the screen and watches the movie. All that you think you are, you are not. All the images in your mind, you are not. All the good and bad, and all the other judgments you make about yourself, you are not. You are not the screen, nor are you the images that appear on it.

But it is possible to have a taste of yourself in reality. Watching the movie of life, you may even see the possibility of letting go of your identification with everything that takes place on the screen. You may see the meaninglessness of the game of life, and the meaningfulness of the taste of your own existence.

You can say yes to what *is*. You and that *is* are one. You become filled with meaning, and everything becomes meaningful. The unifying principle of all that exists becomes apparent. You see that the dignity of Existence cannot be disturbed. You see the unity in diversity.

You fall in love, but this time, it's real love, in which three dimensions of love come together—love for the Source, love for the process of self-development, and love for life as it is. With that love, you can support the growth of your consciousness, which is the real aim and purpose of your life. You can say *"I am,"* but with certainty, because to know reality, one must be real.

Every stick has two ends. Regardless of how long the stick is, even if it's as long as eternity, when you tap anywhere on the stick, the whole stick vibrates. From this, you can see the interrelatedness and interconnectedness of everything that exists.

When you say "this room," what makes it so? The walls and ceiling make it a room. What if you take them away? You can no longer call it a room—you call it a space. You try to define that space by placing some limit, some boundary around it. You may say that space is in San Francisco, for example. Or if you choose a larger scale, you may say that space is in California. But those boundaries are like the walls. If you take them away, what is there? You may choose a bigger boundary—the United States. Or even bigger—planet Earth. Or the solar system, or the Milky Way, or all the galaxies. If you take away all the boundaries, you come to the Timeless Existence of everything that is. You come to one unified Existence.

When you go against the fundamental order of the Universe, you suffer. Every negative state you've had, every negative thought, has its origin in going against that order, and that's why you suffer, until you are ready to see through your wrong way of looking. The same situations keep repeating themselves until you understand what you need to understand.

Transformation means letting go of lies. Things are as they are. By seeing things as they are, you transform into what? Into yourself. That "you," the real you, existed before the universe was manifested. What happens happens, but God never separates from man. The you that exists is not separate from God. No other you can be regarded as permanent. You never were Bob or Lucy or whatever name you have. All of us accept lies as truth. But who you *actually are* does not. Then why is development needed? To let go of extra.

You can't find your existence in the past. You can't find it in the future. When you hear something that has meaning in it, that meaning is you, yourself, in this moment. You're really hearing *I am*. And in that, the entirety supports the entirety, life is giving to life, Existence is manifesting itself.

Everything that appears in time has a Timeless nature. When something returns to its Timeless nature, it's as though it is not. When, from its Timeless nature it manifests in time, it's as though it is.

With this key, you can look at phenomena and understand them better. What is death? It *is* and *is not*. What is birth? *Is* and *is not*. The dynamic of the universe is kinetic. The reality of anything (and everything) is part of the process of Existence—formation and transformation. This is hard to grasp, but easy to experience. Your ideas about yourself are a curtain that separates you from your True nature. If you let go of all of them, you *are*.

In life, which is the wheel of *is* and *is not*, the Absolute exists timelessly, unseparated from everything that is. So you can't experience the Absolute, and *then* experience yourself. The Absolute can only be received in unity.

Becoming familiar with yourself means becoming familiar with how your mind works, and how your body and your feelings function. When you see how they work by observing it in yourself (rather than just hearing about it from outside); when you *experience* it in yourself, it starts to become self-knowledge. Self-knowledge is very important, because it could become Self-understanding.

When self-knowledge connects to the seed of Consciousness that has been given to each of us, it becomes *Being-*knowledge. The fusion of Being and knowledge is your understanding, which is the reality of who you are. You are your understanding.

What we need is to come to the very beginning. You have a body. Bring the mind to it. Then two parts are together. Stay with it until the feelings come in, too. When all three are together, they turn towards your real *I*. When you're connected to that *I*, you receive the emanation of your True nature. That is Consciousness. Consciousness has light, and with it, you can see. You see past the surface appearance of things, to their meaning. Because of that seeing, you become more and more familiar with who you are and what you're supposed to be doing on this Earth. That's the question of everyone who has been here and left, and of everyone who has yet to be born. We are born like a question mark. We are looking to find ourself. We all go through the cycle of birth and death, but there is also the possibility of entering into Timeless Existence.

If you believe you are your body, you don't really exist. We appear on the Earth, and we call that birth. When our time here is over, we call that death. The time between these two events we call our life. Assuming no accident befalls us, we live seventy or eighty years, and each second, the body is subject to a variety of haphazard events that could end its life, because the body is a temporary phenomenon. Then what makes us so important?

You need body-mind connection as long as you are on this Earth. We always need to start at the beginning. The beginning is connection between body and mind. Bringing the mind's attention to your inhalation and exhalation, and staying with it, establishes that connection. This step can't be eliminated. It's needed in every stage of development. We may imagine we're beyond that. But in truth, we never are. We are nothing—temporary creations that appear and disappear! How could someone temporary be so important? Only when we experience our own nothingness are we safe from being crushed by our own ego.

Everything receives its existence moment by moment, from the Source. When you taste *I exist*, that *I* is real because Awareness is giving it reality. When that *I* exists, "you" don't need to know it, because there is no "you." That taste is you—the real you. This is true for any level of direct knowledge—there is no separate "you" to know it. As long as "you" want to know, it means you're stuck in the past or future, so you want the kind of knowing that you can identify with. But to see things as they really are means to see them objectively, without identification.

Existence manifests itself, yet in doing so, doesn't create something separate. When you *exist*, and you eat an apple, what you are really extracting from that apple is yourself. When you are "out of it," you only extract matter and energy to keep this body going, as though the only purpose of eating is to feed the physical body. When you are present, you receive *yourself* in the form of the apple you're eating.

So in the dimension in which you know and taste the unity of yourself *existing*, nothing is happening "out there," because there is no separated "outside." Manifested Existence never separates from unity. The existence of that apple and your existence are one. You *are* that very existence. "You" refers to the *Consciousness*, the knowing that *Existence is*. There really is no separate "you."

Only Existence is. The manifestation of Existence simply indicates *is*. When you really *see* anything, when you *taste* anything, when you really *know* anything, that which you are seeing, knowing, and tasting is in you, and *is* you.

The only thing you can experience in reality is yourself. The reality of all matter, energy, and Consciousness is the Source which manifests it—Awareness. You can only do what Existence does. You can only exist in the same way Existence exists. Knowing this is what makes you real. Without that knowing, "you" refers to something imaginary, something separate, which in reality is not.

75

When you come home to your apartment, you close the door, and maybe even the windows, in order to become a bit free of the hustle and bustle of life. But to come home to your own inner atmosphere, you open all the doors and windows! You become receptive to Conscious energy from the higher aspect of yourself.

We think self-development is difficult. For your personality to develop, of course it's hard—in fact, it's impossible. But it doesn't take energy to exist, to be real. Existence is manifesting, and so, you *are*. When you're connected to that, your consciousness uses the mind as a tool to express Awareness. And your body is Awareness—it constantly gives the taste of its existence as Awareness. To receive that, to know that, you have to *exist*. What does that have to do with you as a personality? Your personality only needs to be in the back seat!

To really understand what makes a building, you can't only look at the materials it's made from. You also need to acknowledge the architect who designed and built it.

To understand the body, we have to do the same thing. We have to acknowledge the intelligence of the Consciousness that put these ingredients together. An architect chooses which materials to use to construct a building. But the architect that builds the body gathers the materials from within itself. So the body is actually nothing other than the light of Consciousness. In fact, everything that is emanated from within the Absolute is light, so everything is made of light. We may look at something as matter or energy or Consciousness. But everything is manifested Awareness.

When you are present, separation disappears. If you look at someone when you're present, you see another aspect of yourself.

79

Clarity brings Love. What you see with real clarity, you can love.

If we actually look, we see we are not living from our human nature. How can you see that? By seeing that your life is ruled by the desires of your body and the desires of your feelings. Your mind is not the boss, because it doesn't work as a mind—it just reacts to your body and feelings. That's why it's always in the past or the future, why it has thoughts but doesn't think.

To fulfill your purpose, your mind has to become a real mind. It has to be in charge of your life. Your mind could be connected to your True nature. Your body and ordinary emotions are your material existence. They can't understand your essential life. But your essential aspect can bring understanding to your material life, so you could be guided by your understanding, not ruled by your physical, mental, and emotional crystallizations (which were formed unconsciously). Those only manifest when *you* don't exist—when your real *I* is not present.

In the absence of vitality, you are ill. Real vitality is a property of your essential part. You have to *exist* in order to properly manage your life energy.

We call ourselves human beings, but are we really? We never learned how to be really human, because we never received a real education, one which supports the growth of our essence. The saying "Know yourself" points to that. But we misunderstand, and think that refers to the story of our life—where we were born, what jobs we've had, where we live....

If someone asks, "Who are you?" and you try to really answer honestly, you can't say one word. Because you don't know yourself. If you see that, you may begin to search for real self-knowledge. If you just take what someone else says as truth, you're back to the story, instead of reality. Reality starts from within—from what you can see and verify in yourself.

"You are the crown of Creation." We've all heard that. But are we truly human? Does that refer to the person who's filled up with false and unverified ideas about himself? To be truly human, we need a Conscious *I*. That *I* is not part of our mind, feelings, or body. But it gives reality to our mind, feelings, and body.

Your mother gave birth to your body, but not to the light that exists within you, the light that was given to you by Existence. The body, like all temporary things, dies, but that light is eternal. It has to be discovered. That's what "know yourself" means. It means *realizing* your Timeless, immortal existence. Heaven and hell are not places—they are dimensions of consciousness. When you *taste* your *existence*, you are in heaven. In the absence of that taste, you are in hell. Body-mind connection is the first step towards heaven, towards coming to your eternal aspect. Because when body and mind remain connected for a while, your real feelings can come in. You become unified within yourself, and you attract Conscious energy—light from your Timeless, eternal nature. With that light, you see things as they are.

To know *I exist* is to know *Existence exists*.

Truth sets you free. Realization is freedom. In each moment, you have a chance to taste your existence. When you actually see something, it means there is something in you that is free from what it sees. Otherwise, you couldn't see it. *Seeing* brings freedom. You don't have to figure out what is. Because it *is*. What *is* is present.

We really don't know the past, even if we think we've experienced it. We try to find it in memory, but at best, that's approximate. Nor can we know the future for certain. Truth can't be found in the past or the future. It's only in the present moment. It's not something to figure out. That's why we don't know ourselves. We want to figure ourselves out. That's not possible. But it is possible to *be* yourself.

There's nothing wrong with thinking, as long as you see you are not your thoughts. The mind has thoughts, but what does that have to do with you? The feelings feel. What do they have to do with you? Your senses have their experience. What does that have to do with you? Those functions are events of life. But you are not an event. You are the Awareness that is aware of events.

When you see that, you can see that you're not this body, so in truth, you're not going to die. The body is a temporary expression of your True nature that appears with your "birth," and eventually disappears. But reality is eternal. What is real always is. Understanding this is freedom, because it's *Self-understanding*. Start at the beginning—breathe, and come to the body. Experience that your body has weight, or that your body has a posture. That brings a little bit of freedom from thoughts.

When you speak about your father, you see him in your mind. Your brother—you see him in your mind. Your home, your mother—anything you say, you see in your mind. But if you say, "God," you can't see God in your mind, but you can experience a presence in your heart. What you see in your mind doesn't actually exist. That which exists—God, Being, Understanding—exists in your heart, not your mind. To really live means living in your heart. Not imagining life in the mind, but *living* life.

Your thoughts are pictures, images on the screen of the mind. But the images are no more real than an image on your computer. Anything you do that brings you to the body, brings you out of the mind, and into life.

The first level of consciousness is being physically asleep. The second level is being psychologically asleep. Being human starts in the third level of consciousness. Being human means *being* human. It means being conscious of your existence, being conscious that you have life.

The fourth level of consciousness is consciousness of unity, being conscious that you exist as an inseparable part of the whole.

To be connected to the fourth level of consciousness, to unity, we need the third level. You have to know you *exist*. Without that, even if you have flashes of the fourth level, you may not even know it. And even if you know it, in the next second, you forget. When you are in the third level, you have an Inner Authority, a real *I*. Then you know. Because real knowing and *being* are one. When you *know*, you *are*. When you *are*, you *know*.

Sometimes we experience being "good"—when we do what we think is right. And we know how fulfilling that is.

But if you make the decision to always be good, you will find out that you can do so only in certain conditions. If the conditions change—for example, if even a tiny bit of criticism is directed at you—you may find yourself doing the opposite of what you intended. When you're happy with the way you act, it's because the conditions are such that you are able to act that way. Our "doing" depends on our conditioning and on the outer conditions at the time, so it can't really be called doing.

We are not in charge of ourselves. What we "do" is just the result of the influence of mass consciousness affecting us. To *do*, you have to be *conscious*. The more you see this, the more it makes sense to pursue a single aim—raising your level of consciousness.

God is constantly giving and forgiving. Real Conscience is the voice of God in us, and is always giving and forgiving.

Unless we develop, we don't have Conscience—what we call conscience is actually related to learned morality mixed with judgments. God is God, and instead of judging you, accepts and forgives everything. God sees Objectively, and in that, there is no good or bad. Good and bad are relative, comparative concepts—something can only be good in relation to something that isn't as good. But whatever you manifest is Existence manifested and manifesting, because you are nothing other than that yourself—Existence being manifested and manifesting.

Whatever you manifest is used—it functions as part of the process. When you manifest in a way that takes you farther away from the taste of harmony, there is some payment, some suffering involved, but that suffering becomes fuel that eventually helps you move towards more harmony. Ultimately, everything that is manifested becomes useful.

Conscience is the taste in your Being that lets you know, before you manifest, how that manifestation will affect your Being. We know what is right, because Conscience is part of our Being. But our real Conscience is asleep, covered over by meaningless sentiment. To be truly alive, to *exist*, is to manifest in harmony with Existence, doing what Existence does, giving and forgiving.

W hen you taste your existence, you don't need anything else. When you have that taste, if someone were to
ask you what you need, it would make you laugh! Because
when you *exist*, everything in the Universe is already
yours, everything is a part of you.

To really live life, you need to say "Yes!"—you need gusto. And that comes from inner balance. Sometimes, just the thought of it connects you. Sometimes you have to work for it by bringing body and mind together and allowing them to stay together. You use the breath to keep them together for a while, until your feelings come in. When these three aspects work in harmony, you have gusto. You don't let life pass you by. Instead, you *receive* life, so you can receive something from it. When the postman delivers a package, you need to be home to receive it. But if you catch yourself, you see that you are always somewhere else. You didn't choose to go there, but your mind takes you there. The influence of mass consciousness moves you like hay in the wind.

Yet, if you see that, you are lucky. Because every possibility for movement in the right direction comes from *seeing*. Don't turn away from anything you could see about yourself. You don't need to be identified with what you see, because whatever you see is not you. You can't see that which is actually you. Anything you say about yourself is about what you are *not*. But if you see often enough that "I'm not this and I'm not that…," you may also see that you *are*. Not *who* you are (because that, you can't see) but that you *are*.

"Who am I?" You could search forever, but you will never find that "who." If you are able to receive the taste of your existence, you find out that you are not what you see, not what you touch, not what you hear, or say. In fact, you are not anything in the entire manifested universe. You are the

Awareness that is *aware* of the manifested universe. Your eyes can see everything, but they can't see themselves. You can observe everything, but not yourself. Why not? Because you find your Being in *being* yourself. "Who am I?" The "who" is somewhere "out there." That's what we imagine. But in *I am*, there is no "who," only Existence. And the *taste* of it gives real, *essential* satisfaction.

But taste is here and then a moment later, it's gone. You have to renew it. Moment after moment, you have to follow the taste of your existence—*I am*. That's the remedy for ignorance and suffering.

Our mind doesn't want to know the Truth. It prefers to hear philosophy about it. We are usually satisfied with philosophy, because we imagine we've learned something. But the Truth puts your mind out of business. And nobody wants that. If you want your mind to stay in business, at least have a *good* business! Come to the body and know body breathes and body has weight on the ground. Work with the Nine Principles of Harmony.

There are two ends of this stick. On one end, you take yourself to be this body. So you have to work to bring body and mind together, again and again and again. On the other end of the stick, you take yourself to be Existence. And for that to really be so, you have to let go of everything, and accept your nothingness. Actually, your no-*thing*-ness. That means you are not this body, mind, or feelings. It's said that when Buddha was asked, "Who are you?" the only thing he said was "I am awake." When you *are*, you have a chance to know the meaning and purpose of Existence, the meaning and purpose of your life.

Your body is always doing something. But if you aren't connected to it, you have no idea what it's doing. Your body is sitting. Are you experiencing that? Your body is breathing. Are you experiencing that? Your body is reading. Instead of letting your body be separate, you could be with it.

Before you invest in buying a house, you want to know as much as you can about it. How is the foundation? Are the walls insulated? What kind of windows does it have?

Your body is also a house, and you're spending a lot more than money on it. You're spending your life energy! But what do you know about it? Unless you have a relationship to your body, you end up misusing the energy you receive from food, from the air you breathe, and from the impressions you take in.

If you really want to know about your house, you have to live in it. When you bring your mind to your body, you begin to fulfill your purpose.

You may go to Central Park for an afternoon, but you don't say, "That's *my* park." Your house is not really yours, either. Neither is your body. You may be in it for eighty years, but then you come out of it again. Eighty years is nothing! You live on the Earth for a while, and then you go back to the earth, to the ground. So does the Earth belong to you, or you to it?

You can *have* form, but you can't *have* meaning. Meaning doesn't enter the word "have." It enters the word "am."

"I have" relates to form. "I am" relates to Being. To relate to the word "Being," you need to *be*. You can't have the Truth. The requirement for entering into the Truth is to taste the truth of your existence. To be conscious of anything, you have to be conscious of your own existence.

Knowing and Being

You *exist*. This has to become so much a part of you, that you never doubt it. It doesn't depend on whether you know it or not, or whether you're asleep or not. The parts exist because of the whole. But the whole does not exist because of the parts. The *I* you refer to when you say "I" can only be the Totality. If you are referring to something else, that something is imaginary. First there is *is*, and then *is* expresses itself in endless ways.

You think you see your body. You think you see others. But we don't really see anything! You imagine others. You imagine your body. Unless you first come to *is*, what can you see? Nothing.

We see life "on the screen," outside of us, because we are "outside," and "looking" from outside. Of course, outer events are mesmerizing. Of course we get caught up in them. And we are afraid of everything—everything makes us shrink. When you have body-mind connection, you are on the line which is connected to the *I* via taste. Then you don't have to be afraid of things. When you come to *I exist*, you see everything inside yourself, because you, yourself are "inside," included in the *is*, not outside in imaginary existence. Your Being has to be in what you're formulating or manifesting—then it is real.

The Truth is true for you when you are *being* Truth—because then you are in it, and it is in you.

If you are interested in seeing things as they really are, there is some good news—you can only see things as they really are! There is no other way of seeing! Seeing things as they really are means *seeing*. If you *see*, you see things as they really are.

We don't really see. Instead, we see the image of what we look at. We see our interpretation of it. We filter every-thing through our associations from the past and our ideas about the future. We don't actually *see* anything, because we constantly misuse our senses! We immediately inter-pret what they take in, and get lost in the interpretation.

Before we can work with this situation, we have to see that we mechanically associate, interpret, and have commen-tary about everything without ever having decided to do that. It's not even you who does that—it's your acquired mind, not your own mind. It's the mind of mass con-sciousness.

Thoughts come and go, and you are not in charge of them. It's as though you've given your mind to thousands of strangers, who come and go without paying you rent, and even damage your space.

We have a book of memories collected from the stories of our life, and we always try to improve our stories, and jus-tify our behavior—"I wasn't so bad…it wasn't really my fault…." We constantly try to polish our self-image. And no matter how much we try, we don't succeed, because that person doesn't really exist! The person you imagine yourself to be is just a thought, or a feeling, or a sensation. Yet we collect those stories as though they are the treasures of our life. We are delighted when someone listens to our stories. And of course, we modify and color them, to make them look a little better.

You can see it for yourself. You can see where your attention goes. As soon as you wake up tomorrow, look and see where your attention goes. Immediately, you are in the past, or having some anxiety about the future, so you don't even experience getting out of bed. The experiencer is asleep. What can you do about it? Nothing! You cannot change anything about yourself. If you push something to the side, it just appears again at another time.

But with enough desire to pay for the Truth, and with the ability to pay for it, we can find a way. The direction is to accept what you see. Acceptance gives you energy, and that energy becomes your capital. Acceptance is not self-justification. Nor does it look at things in terms of opposites. It's in a dimension above past and future, so it sees both sides simultaneously. Once you see your intelligence and your ignorance each exist in their own dimension, there is no reason to be jealous of others, or to hate. When you are in the dimension of intelligence, your ignorance doesn't interfere with it. You simply see through it. When you look from a higher dimension, what you see in lower dimensions becomes transparent—you see through it.

To be able to see things as they really are, the requirement is to see yourself as you are. When you do, whoever or whatever you see is included. There is no separation.

To *be*, we only need to let go of imaginary separation. Being means eternal Being, without beginning or end. Being always *is*. Moment after moment, we receive our *is-ness*. Moment after moment, we exist in unity. Our relative life comes and goes, but what underlies it is Timeless Awareness.

Everything has the same Timeless nature, but you and I are not the same, nor are we the same as a glass or a chair. Without particularity, without each thing having a particular form, there is no Absolute either. Unless we realize that, we are not seeing reality. If we minimize the importance of particularity by saying that everything is constantly transformed by the Law of Constant Change, we are not seeing that something has to exist to change constantly.

Without particularity, we are looking at the Absolute as a timeless shell which envelops time, but we are not seeing what is *within* the Absolute, what its inner dynamic is. Of course, this hand is a hand because it's part of the body, and the body is part of the Totality, but we shouldn't forget that this hand is a *hand*. It is not an eye and cannot be an eye. It is not separate from the whole, but it is exactly that which it is and cannot be anything else—it occupies an exact position and fulfills an exact function in the Totality.

What is the meaning of magic? Look at Existence. There is not one thing that is not magic. You put one wheat berry into the ground, and the soil gives you fifty wheat berries! Look at the color of a flower. How did the Earth produce that? Look at an oak tree—the entire tree is contained in one acorn! Not one thing exists that isn't *given*. We can't create something out of nothing—everything is already here. Your body is made of trillions of cells, created from the food you eat that was produced by the Earth. Look at what Existence does, compared to your part in creating a child. That's the magnitude of Existence. And still, we say, "my daughter, my son." The enormity and the majesty of the Absolute cannot be comprehended by us—not any aspect of it.

And in this incredible universe, look at what Existence has come up with to create us—our eyes, for example. They are alive and can see life around us. We make glasses to cover the eyes, which can make what the eyes see appear bigger, but the glasses cannot see, cannot be alive, cannot comprehend.

We can combine matter and energy and make a robot, but it's not alive and can't comprehend. We can make a chip, and put tons of information into it, so it performs a function. But we were created "empty," capable of gathering and building everything we need in order to understand the cosmos. Look at this potential we were created with, and you can see to what extent we ignore our possibilities and misuse our position in the universe.

Experiencing that your body is breathing and that your body has weight is a way to enter into any of the Nine Principles. Look at Body Comfortable, for example. How are you going to get comfortable? How are you going to deal with all your thoughts and emotions? It looks impossible. But you begin to register your breathing. With each inhalation and exhalation, you enter more deeply into Body Comfortable. When you come to a taste of Body Comfortable, you understand that the body isn't what you assumed it is. It's something that connects you to your existence and to everything that exists.

oment after moment, life exists. Moment after moment, the interconnectedness of all that exists is renewed afresh. The desire to *know* and the desire to *be* are emissaries from our True nature. An impression of our existence is received in Consciousness. Consciousness is a light with which we can see. *Seeing, Being,* and *knowing* all refer to the same thing—and show us Existence exists, *I* exist, the body exists.

Everything that exists has a particular level of consciousness. To raise your level of consciousness is to move towards who you really are. When we look from time, there's effort and movement. But from the Timeless, no effort is involved. The Light of Awareness does not use force to travel. What we think of as light, what we think of as energy, is "reflected light," not *light* itself. Reflected light is relative Existence, the observable universe. But in the *realizable* universe, in Awareness, in reality itself, no energy is needed. *Everything* is real. The sun gives light to millions of homes, but there is one sun. There is one life— appearing in many different forms. There are many ways that point to the Truth. But when you come to the Truth, they become one for you, because they are all pointing to the same thing. To be in the moment is to know yourself. Everything that we wish exists in *this* moment.

You're standing in a meadow at night. You turn on your flashlight, and it shows the path. In your life, your consciousness is that flashlight. All the steps you need to take to stay on that path, and also, knowing why you are walking on it and where is it that you wish to go to—what your *aim* is—all of that is the work of Conscience. If you really wish to know how to live your daily life, both Consciousness and Conscience are needed.

In the ordinary consciousness that we have in our daily life, there is no real Conscience. That's why people turn against each other, and life on the Earth is often hell. If Conscience were manifesting on Earth, the Earth wouldn't be called Earth anymore. It would be called heaven.

Our ordinary thinking is passive and drains our energy. We don't choose the thoughts we have. If fact, those thoughts aren't even our own. They come from outside, from "others."

But it is possible to think in a way that increases our vital energy. Those thoughts make us more radiant, more alive.

When you're conscious of your existence, your thoughts are elevated. And they are your own—they come to you from your Timeless nature. They relate to the meaning and purpose of life. They support you to raise your level of consciousness, and bring you more and more understanding. Realizations come from your Timeless nature. Your *Being* participates in them and you *taste* reality.

A photograph of the ocean indicates that there is an ocean. But no matter how long you look at it, you don't experience its magnitude. You don't smell it or experience its depth, its warmth, or the waves.

Our mind is the same as that photo. In our mind, we don't see the actual thing. We see a photo, an image of something. So of course, whatever we "see" in the mind doesn't have life.

It's been said that God created man out of a lump of clay, but man didn't have life. So God gave light to that clay, and it became Adam. Now look at yourself—you are asleep. Then you remember you are part of the whole of Existence—you see yourself in light. You become alive. But that light didn't come to you from outside. Before that moment, you were looking at yourself, and in fact, at everything, with your mind. That means you weren't seeing yourself—you were looking at a picture, an image, a concept of yourself. When you see *yourself*, instead of the picture, it seems like you've *become* alive, but really, you are always alive, always in light. When you're asleep, you don't know it.

If there was only empty space, only nothingness, Existence would be cold. The brilliant diversity of form in endless exchange and interaction gives warmth to Existence. It's as though the Absolute is a painter who enjoys creating this infinite beauty. And into each form, from the largest down to the very atoms that everything is made of, he puts some of his emanation, so what is created can also create by manifesting.

Because God *sees* us, we have the possibility to *see*. We can do the same thing God does, in miniature. God *sees* everything, and so, gives everything life.

Everyone and everything is affected by *seeing*, because *seeing* shines a light on what is seen. In order to *see*, you need a real *I*. You need a real *I* to see the Timeless nature of things. Without it, you hear the Truth in your mind, as an explanation. Then, the most you can do is picture it, and if it "makes sense," you accept it. Or you may just accept it on faith. But if you have a real *I*, your Consciousness *sees* with the Light of Awareness, and brings existence to what you see.

To move from complication to simplicity means to move from what you've acquired (which is what you are not), to yourself, to your very Being.

You are sitting in a room. That space is always here. That's the real meaning of "here." The walls of the room are temporary, and they define the space, so we can call it a room.

Words are like walls. They are temporary containers that give definition to the meaning inside them. They don't give or create the meaning. They are just containers of the meaning you put in them. They contain the meaning only temporarily. If you are not connected to the meaning, the words are like an empty room.

The word "I" is the same. When you say it, you express whatever meaning is inside the "room" you're calling "I." It depends on your level of consciousness in that moment. Your real *I* is an expression of your *I am-ness*. And the more you become connected to the meaning, the more you see that the "I" is not its own separate entity. It is Existence expressing itself both through and as that *I*.

Nothing real ever disappears. Everything that was, *is.* And everything that will be, *is.*

Your past is real. When it took place, it took place in the moment. If you want to find your past now, you have to come to this moment, because that's the only place your past actually is. Your future is also real, but it exists in this moment.

To understand the moment, you have to *be* in the moment. To understand yourself, you need to *be* yourself.

When we enter into the *is-ness* of anything, we enter into the *is-ness* of the Totality.

A poet said: "There is a cup made of ice, filled with snow, floating in a lake, and it is raining."

But all of that is water. What is form? Flowers, trees, people—everything that exists is Awareness! Awareness, manifesting as Awareness, Consciousness, energy, and matter. The fact that there are forms shows that these four dimensions exist.

We think that freedom means not being subject to any law. But the Universe couldn't exist without its Laws, which apply always and everywhere. There is an order and purpose and meaning to Existence. If we were free to do whatever we wanted to, we might see that we don't really know what to do. To be free, we need knowledge—knowledge that's complete.

We are not free—because we are fragmented and subject to many different influences. The person who wishes for freedom has to make himself free from some of those influences. We do things according to our conditioned, crystallized, habitual ways of reacting. To wish to not be totally subject to your crystallized behavior, to not automatically react to everything that comes in front of you— that is a good aim! So you have to learn about yourself. You need to understand yourself, at least enough to know how to not have a severe reaction to every little thing.

We constantly serve our conditioning, our habits, our acquired thought patterns and feelings. But the less we serve these unconscious influences, and the more we serve higher purposes, the freer we are, and the less subject we are to lower dimensions.

Your level of Being determines what you serve, and what serves your development and gives you the possibility to understand yourself. Freedom isn't just a word, just an attractive concept. You have to pay for freedom. To the extent you understand yourself, you are free.

What is understanding? To explain understanding, we first have to look at two other words—information and knowledge.

Information needs only to be put into your mind. That's sufficient for it to do its job. Knowledge is information that's been intentionally examined from a variety of angles, until our logical mind is satisfied with its soundness. That's one aspect of knowledge. Knowledge also has a practical side. It has to be applied in your daily life and put into practice. Then you can really call it knowledge.

But no matter how much knowledge you acquire, it doesn't give you even a grain of understanding. Something more is needed—Being. The light of Being turns knowledge into understanding.

Everything in our life is so temporary. But reality is permanent and unchangeable. Our physical, mental, and emotional desires all come from the body, our temporary aspect, which is subject to the Law of Constant Change. And those desires are precisely what hinder our growth. Fortunately, there is a line that connects the permanent and the temporary. That's the line of self-development, and from it comes real spirituality, real science, and real philosophy. When we become interested in self-development, we begin to see and understand our desires.

The process of formation and transformation is always taking place, and so everything that appears must disappear. Everything that's born must also die. But whatever is transformed into a deeper, more essential dimension of itself doesn't actually die. That's why constant self-development is needed.

Millions of transformations take place inside a plant to enable it to produce a flower. Millions of transformations take place for a lump of coal to become a diamond. And countless transformations are needed for someone to become conscious. In each moment of our lives, we are transforming food, air, and most importantly, impressions. If we are able to take in impressions consciously, we see things as they really are.

We cannot understand even the simplest physical laws when we live in the dimension of mechanical consciousness. Reality can be understood only by coming to a level of consciousness that sees that everything comes from the Source.

When you look with your mind, you don't see the tree you're looking at. You see its name and your description of its outer form.

But when you look with Consciousness, you see the tree as it is—in the moment. You see the *existence* of the tree. The Totality is always present. With Consciousness, you don't just see name and form. You see something magical. You see the presence of the Absolute in the tree. You see that presence as the tree.

That presence is always here, but our ability to receive it varies. We each receive it in varying degrees, according to our level of consciousness.

Your mind has the ability to remind you of what you wish to do, but it doesn't have the power to get you to do it, because will is needed. But we can't acquire will unconsciously, mechanically. Real will is connected to our True nature.

To be able to do what you understand, to live the way your understanding directs you to, you have to be connected to a higher dimension of consciousness. Bringing your mind to the activity of your body is a good way to start.

You can't rely on knowing. Knowing is not understanding. Your understanding can express itself as knowing, but understanding has to be there first.

The most important aspect of development is *seeing*. You should be grateful for whatever you see of yourself. It doesn't matter what you see. When you *see*, something takes place in your inner world. You begin to discover your psychological landscape. Eventually, you have to know that country well enough to want an Inner Authority, a real *I*, to bring order to it, for the benefit of all.

If, over a long period of time, you accept what you see of yourself without criticism, something fundamental changes in you.

But we don't see, because we learned to think instead of seeing. And we don't recognize the difference. We think we are seeing when we're only thinking. When you're critical of what you "see," you're not seeing, you're thinking. In seeing, there is joy, because seeing is in a higher dimension. When your seeing is in the line of development, you see your own falsity. When your seeing is in the Timeless line, you see what you truly are, what you are in reality. You see you are not separated from your True nature, that you have never been separated from Unity, that separation is only a thought. Everything is actually created by the Absolute, within the Absolute, in order to fulfill the purpose of the Absolute. There is only one Existence, and at all times, you are actually in harmony with the totality of everything that exists.

Knowing and Being

With thoughts, you look only at your superficial aspect—
at the debris on the surface of the ocean. You don't see
things as they are. Seeing is like brushing the debris
away—you see clear water. You see yourself reflected. And
you know that you are the consciousness that sees, not the
image.

The ability to think is one thing. The ability to *see* is another. The ability to be conscious of what you think and what you see is yet another dimension. That lets you think and see with clarity, because you know you are connected to both ends of the stick—to your Timeless nature and your temporary nature. You know where you are on the scale of Existence.

Don't let go of what you already know how to do. Once you know how to come to body-mind connection, you need to keep that clarity all your life. That's always the starting point, no matter what dimension of consciousness you reach.

God (the Absolute, Awareness, the Unifying Principle of Existence) is hidden in everything that exists—inside every atom! You can *see* God, *experience* God, but not with your physical eyes—with actual *seeing*.

What is real is always present. You can't find it in the past and you can't find it in the future. It always exists—in the Moment.

The observable and the realizable are actually one. But you can also observe, also see, the realizable, to the degree that you have real understanding. Whatever is higher than your current understanding, you cannot observe, but as you develop, you may at some time be able to.

When we are not present, we don't actually make deci-sions. Outer conditions make them for us!

In different periods, Teachings rooted in Truth sprout in different ways. The explanation, the "ladder" that people can use to climb from mass consciousness to the threshold of the actual Truth, is different in different periods of the Earth. But the esoteric aspect, the deeper reality they point to, is unchanging.

Truth doesn't talk to your personality. It doesn't acknowledge non-existence as Existence. When it uses the word "you," it's not addressing your personality, because, as something separate from the whole, you don't exist.

Meaning unifies. Without meaning, we get lost in diversity. Moving towards meaning brings us towards unity.

In the line of past and future, we change our thoughts, but there is no movement in consciousness. We remain in the same level. The line of development refers to movement in our level of consciousness. The Timeless line is *Awareness* manifesting in the moment.

There's a huge difference between thinking and having thoughts. In thinking, there's a thinker. Thoughts have no thinker. Thoughts are like passengers in a taxi. They make you go wherever they want. But there's a difference—they don't tip you. Actually, they take something from you.

Purposeful thinking gives you energy. Having thoughts drains your energy. You have thoughts when your mind is passive. Passivity drains your energy. Thinking is active. Thinking has the potential to bring you to receptivity. Then, instead of "thinking" just by focusing on something, you think, then you receive. You think, and some new perspective, some new clarity comes to you. You gain a little bit of wisdom.

The Universe worked hard to create an instrument as fine as the human being. But that refers to a real human being, not to us as we are. It means *being* human. It doesn't mean this reactive automaton. It doesn't mean this person who is at the mercy of every outer influence and doesn't know who he is. We constantly think we are the personality we acquired from our upbringing. This mistaken identity is the cause of our suffering. We move through life blindly because we are afraid to ask ourselves: "What is the purpose of Existence?" "Why was I born?" "What's the meaning of my life?" We are afraid to search for the meaning.

To have a correct picture, we have to see there are two universes, the observable and the realizable. We've lost the ability to realize, so we are disconnected from reality. Reality belongs to the realizable universe. Real love belongs to the realizable universe. Real knowledge—knowledge of the part and the whole—belongs to the realizable universe. The meaning of your life belongs to the realizable universe.

When we lose connection to the realizable, we take appearances to be reality. Look at how disappointing it is when someone looks at you and takes your outer appearance to be you. There is form and there is meaning. Meaning and form have to be experienced together.

The time that we measure by the clock, and divide into weeks, years, centuries, and millennia is passing time. It "begins" somewhere and "goes" somewhere. There is also existing time. "Was" or "will be" don't apply to it. Only *is* applies. Existing time is in the present moment, and the present moment contains the entire past and future. Existing time refers to meaning. Meaning is fundamental—it exists, independent of time and space. There is one Timeless Moment, which is the reality of Existence, ever-present.

We identify with the observable universe, so we don't understand time. When we go through the day mechanically, with our automatic assumptions and expectations, we are not available to experience what is in the moment. But every now and then, we may have one small experience, one instant in which we enter into reality. Your body, your mind, and your feelings live in passing time. But the reality of yourself is not in passing time—it's in the Timeless Moment.

Nothing separates you from reality except your thoughts, which you draw automatically from your conditioning by mass consciousness. Actually, there's no problem with those thoughts except for your identification with them!

Only Existence exists. Existence doesn't see problems. It sees you as you are. In that seeing, you exist, your body exists, and even your thoughts are included. Everything is real.

But we forget what makes everything real, and we imagine that reality is in each thing as a separate thing. So we see things, but we don't see them as they really are. Things are real when you see they're connected to their Source. If you really look at yourself, you see Existence.

How do you get something you want? If you want to eat, you need money. So you get a job. With the money you earn, you buy your food. We all understand that. But when we want something of real value, something connected to the meaning of our life, we forget that we need to pay for it.

If you say, "I wish to *know* I have a body," you're actually saying, "I wish to *own* a body," because only when you really know you have a body do you actually have one! Isn't that as important as having a car? And look at how long you work to get a car. That's why it's difficult for us to have anything real—we forget about the payment. Of course, if you're lucky, your parents may buy you a car. But no one, not even the Creator, can give you something real, because that would contradict the Universal Laws. If you want something real, you have to pay for it yourself.

If you think that your life on this Earth can give you what you want, if you think you can get away from the struggle of living, get free from pain and suffering, you're making a big mistake! Because that's not why we've been given life. Life is like climbing a mountain. With each new step there are new difficulties. If you think "Why me? My neighbor doesn't have this problem," you're not looking at things correctly.

A more useful attitude is this: "There must be a purpose in experiencing this difficulty. I wish to know that purpose. I want to understand why I'm dissatisfied, why my relationships don't go the way I wish, why my health isn't what I wish it to be, why I'm not able to help others and support life the way I wish to."

If you wish to understand this, you may discover that every difficulty has been given to you to use as a stepping stone. When you start using them that way, you become grateful. You see how benevolent Existence is in taking you on this difficult road, where every step can bring you face to face with your own nothingness, with your inability to do. Seeing this in acceptance is using it as a stepping stone. The bottom line is, our level of Being has to change. And this doesn't happen by itself, or by trying to surround yourself with easy conditions.

There was a poet who wrote, "I'm bothered by those who admire me and think I'm somebody. Where is that precious adversary who brings my face to the mud, and makes me take a hard look at myself? Who am I really? What's the meaning of my life?"

These questions don't arise when we're lying on a bed of roses.

What to do with all this? If you really want to do something, choose something very small that you know you can fulfill—like bringing your mind to the fact of the body inhaling, or the body moving, one time each day. Little by little, you can add to that. The key is to decide on something and carry it through—for yourself. There's no one to applaud you—you are facing only yourself. If you dare to face yourself, you will see many things you don't like. If you see them in acceptance, you will begin to also see aspects of yourself that have not been spoiled by the outside world. You may begin, for the first time in life, to separate the wheat from the chaff—to distinguish Truth from falsity. This is the key to freedom.

When you go to the past, you get lost in it. But your past experiences could support your growth, if your aim is to bring them to the present. Each event from your past, when you understand it, becomes something you can use. Understanding doesn't mean going to the past and getting lost in it. It means shining the light of the Moment on the past, so you can *see*.

Trying to change your personality is like trimming the branches of a tree without having any understanding of its roots. You don't know what you're doing or what the result will be. That's why your direction should be to accept your personality fully.

When you have understanding, you consider the whole in relation to whatever you're doing. You can never bring real improvement unless you fully understand the whole. There are a million things that need to be taken into consideration in making even the smallest change. So don't try to change things. Instead, look for understanding of what *is,* as it is.

Self-development has two processes that go hand in hand. One is discovery. Bit by bit, you discover how unconscious you are.

The other process is uncovering. Little by little, you see there is something essential in you. It's covered up, hidden, but it's still there, and still intact. Through discovery, you see the part of yourself that you've acquired—your personality. Through uncovering, you see the part of you that was given to you by Existence—your essence. The more you discover and uncover, the more you see that your possibilities for development are with your essence. Then, instead of trying to fix your personality, which has been conditioned by the outer world, you wish to accept it for what it is.

We take ourselves to be important. But we aren't. We worry about death as something that's going to happen, but it already happened! When we don't *know* we exist, we're dead! We think we have many wonderful qualities. But do we? We need to see through our imaginary self-image. We begin to see our personality for what it really is, and to accept (rather than trying to "fix") what we see, because the only thing we need is to uncover our essential part, and support it to grow.

Your body is always doing something, but almost always without the support of your mind and feelings. When you're putting on your clothes, or washing your face, or eating, your mind and feelings are occupied with other things. Their energy is wasted. If the mind stays with the body, the energy that it saves could be used to gain direction and clarity for your life. Then, if the feelings also become connected, their energy can create a supportive harmony for you. You are not so identified with everything, and you don't have to look to others for acknowledgment.

How do you take good care of something? By *being* with it. That's how a mother takes care of her child.

When you have a clear direction and know you are moving towards it, you have self-respect. In a small way, you can see this when you do things as well as you can. When you want to get your sink as clean as possible, and you do it, you feel some sense of satisfaction. That feeling is simple, but it's very valuable. Without enough of this type of satisfaction, we look for satisfaction in ways that are both damaging and unfulfilling.

Moment after moment, Existence is manifesting itself, and moment after moment, gives us a chance to be present.

How amazing to see Existence participating in this physical dimension! You can support its participation in the activity of your body by having body-mind connection.

Evil appears in the absence of reality. The root of evil is ignorance. And the root of ignorance is being ignorant of who we are. In other words, not knowing you *exist*. Ignorance creates fear. To be ignorant means to ignore that you have life, ignore that the body is so temporary and that life is eternal, ignore the interconnectedness of everything that exists.

But when you really know you exist, you don't do evil.

When you know you need help, you become responsible. What is your responsibility? To be receptive to the support that is given to you. When you allow yourself to receive that support, you also gain the ability to help.

Real consciousness begins in the level that is free from the mind—in the level where there are no thoughts.

The purpose of watching your mind is to acquire the ability to leave it alone, to let the mind be. When you let it be, you have a chance to see you are not your mind. You are not your thoughts. Then the mind can do what it does without disturbing you, because what's actually bothering you is not your mind, but your identification with it as yourself.

Your thoughts and feelings are happening to you. But you are not those thoughts or feelings. You put clothes on your body, but you don't imagine that they're you. You put on different clothes every day. Your thoughts and feelings change every minute! They're just passersby. They come and they go.

If you ask yourself "Who am I? What am I?" you may come up with many things to say about yourself. But none of them are satisfactory to your innermost being. You're Mr. or Ms. So and So. This is where you live. This is your job. Those are just descriptions of life, but not life itself. You are life itself.

You may have become a doctor, a lawyer, or an engineer. But that's just a label you've been given, an identity. Is the university your creator? In order to really *live* your life, you have to *be*. First you have to *be*. Then you can learn other things. But first you need to know who you really are.

Our thoughts, our feelings, in fact, everything about us is a curtain that separates us from the source of our existence. We need to open the curtain and see our connection to our Timeless nature. To open the curtain, we don't need to get rid of anything. We simply need to not misinterpret things. When we don't misinterpret things, we don't identify with them. And when we're not identified, we can see the nature of reality.

The ocean is formed by the rivers that flow into it. But when the rivers flow into the ocean, they lose their "riverness." They're just part of the ocean. In the same way, we are just drops in the ocean of Existence. When you enter the ocean, you lose your "drop-ness." You let go of your identification with yourself. We have to open our mind and feelings, and allow them to see the bigger picture. Then we can correctly place ourselves.

Yesterday and tomorrow only have existence in today, and today is the reality of this moment. The moment offers us the only possibility we have to actualize our potential.

Everything is of the same substance, which is light itself. The nature of Existence is light. Everything that exists expresses its existence, and so, everything is connected.

Separation is imaginary and only brings suffering. Existence is always in unity.

Our reactions create a fog that doesn't let us see things as they are.

When something "bad" happens, you could ask yourself: "What does it really mean? What does it mean in relation to my life?" Say, for example, you lost a thousand dollars. Instead of just reacting negatively, you could look and see that the things you value the most can't be taken from you. That's something useful you can do with your mind. Your feelings can also support you when you're present—nothing from the past or future affects them. They help you to see that the events that take place are outside—they're not inside you, so you don't need to let them affect you so much. Another thing you can do is to accept that you may have somehow been the cause of what happened. Then you can look and see what you can do in order not to have the same or similar experience. That way, you may be more able to forgive the other people involved.

But the best way to deal with events is to see that everything that happens is a gift if you use it to bring you to the present, to your body. Your body breathes. No one can take that away from you, as long as you're alive. When your mind stays with your body inhaling and exhaling, room is created for Consciousness to enter. You can experience the joy of knowing you have life. With that, you can deal with things more constructively. Whatever your body does, be present with it. When your body eats, be present with it. When it walks, be present with it. When your body is talking, be with it. If you're present with your body, you find everything that happens supports your growth.

In reality, you don't exist. Your body doesn't exist. But Existence exists! That's your True nature. When you come to your True nature, you have a real *I*, so you exist. When you have a real *I*, you have a real body. What makes your *I* and your body real? They are real when you *see*, when you *taste* that they are made of Awareness, and unseparated from Awareness as the Totality.

There are many things we know are good for us, but we don't do them. And there are many things we know aren't good for us, but we still do them. Why is that? The answer is that even what we know, we don't fully understand.

When you really understand you should do something, you do it. And when you really understand you shouldn't do something, you don't. There are many things we could understand if we truly wished to. The problem is that we were taught that we could understand just with our mind, just by thinking. But thoughts are just thoughts. Real understanding is the union of knowing and Being.

We always look for something outside of ourselves. We go from book to book, class to class, teacher to teacher. But we don't know what we're looking for.

You don't know it, but you're really searching for yourself. You want to know your existence. You have a hard time finding it because you limit it. Your existence is Timeless, boundless, and permanent. But you think it's temporal, something you can look at and name. There's nothing wrong with looking at things as they appear to be, as long as you don't separate them from their Absolute nature. You have to taste the reality of yourself, which is free from time and space. Then you can also look at your temporary nature without getting lost.

Whenever you can, look at things with "better eyes." That means seeing things from a higher level of consciousness. That helps you and the world around you. You may not know how to do that, but if you keep that wish alive in yourself, it begins to help you. You may become more open to receive finer consciousness.

We connect to the body in order to know *there is a body.* We know *there is a body* in order to come to the *I* that knows that the body exists. We remain with that *I* in order to know *I exist in unity.* This is why we do Breema— we come to the body to come to *I exist,* and from *I exist* to our Timeless nature.

If you have a moment in which everything becomes clear, and the light of Consciousness penetrates every aspect of you, why should that be the only moment? Why couldn't you have another moment?

BREEMA

Being

Right now

Everywhere

Every moment

Myself

Actually

The Breema Center

Since 1980, the Breema Center has been presenting Breema's practical approach to harmony and Self-understanding. The world headquarters for practitioner and instructor certification and continuing education, the Center also gives classes, workshops, and intensives for students of all levels. People come from all over the world, attracted by Breema's philosophy, principles, bodywork, and exercises. Studying at the Center, they find essential support in creating a new, unified relationship between the body, mind, and feelings, and in bringing greater harmony and presence to their lives.

The Breema Center maintains an active relationship with certified practitioners and instructors, and an up-to-date international directory of instructors and practitioners, plus listings of Breema classes and presentations worldwide. Information is available on our website, by phone, mail, or email.

THE BREEMA CENTER
Jon Schreiber, D.C., Director
6076 Claremont Avenue
Oakland, CA 94618

510-428-0937
email: center@breema.com
website: breema.com

The Breema Clinic

We have been using Breema bodywork, Self-Breema exercises, and working with the principles of Breema since 1981 to support people to experience greater well-being, harmony, and essential interest in life. Receiving Breema and practicing Self-Breema support the unification of body, mind, and feelings. As these three come together, they begin to function naturally, and we become receptive to finer consciousness. This becomes our entry to real health, which means harmony with Existence.

THE BREEMA CLINIC
Jon Schreiber, D.C., Director
6201 Florio Street
Oakland, CA 94618

510-428-1234
email: clinic@breema.com
website: breemahealth.com

Jon Schreiber

Jon Schreiber is the director of the Breema Center, which presents the transformational tools of Breema, Self-Breema, and the Nine Principles of Harmony. He is also the founder and director of the Breema Clinic, which supports people to move in the direction of real health. Since 1980 he has been teaching at the Breema Center, as well as nationally and inter-nationally, and is the author of many books on the philosophy, principles, and practice of Breema.

Books from The Breema Center
in print, eBook, & audio CD format
Available from local and online bookstores

BREEMA *and the Nine Principles of Harmony*   – by Jon Schreiber

Breema is universal and has great potential value to anyone with a sincere interest in Truth, because it's a practical road to Self-understanding. Breema's timeless principles are applicable to every situation in life, and they open us to the possibility of awakening to the essential unity of Existence in this very moment.

available in print, audio, and eBook format
print: hardcover, 168 pages,
    7" x 9", 81 photos • $25
audio: 2-CD set,
    read by Jon Schreiber • $20

Every Moment Is Eternal:
The Timeless Wisdom of Breema   – by Jon Schreiber

This book talks to our essential nature, because Truth already exists there. The more our essence is nurtured, the greater the chance that cracks may appear in our conditioned attitude towards life. Through these cracks, we may see things we haven't seen before, and nourish our essential desire for Self-understanding.

available in print and eBook format
print: hardcover, 208 pages, 4.5" x 6" • $15

Freedom Is in This Moment: *365 Insights for Daily Life*
– by Jon Schreiber

When you read these writings, you are filled up with an inner resonance, because their reality and meaning are in you as well as all around you. When you hear the Truth, you also hear it inside of yourself, in your very essence. The Truth is not something foreign. It's already part of you just because you exist!

available in print and eBook format
print: hardcover, 448 pages, 4.5" x 6" • $18.95

Freedom Comes from Understanding:
Insights for Meaningful Life

– by Jon Schreiber

How does Existence support you? By letting you know you belong. When you become conscious of your own existence, that Consciousness is the beginning of connection to your Timeless nature.

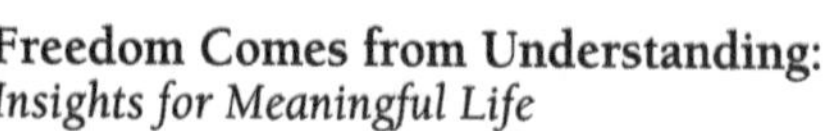

available in print, audio, and eBook format
print: hardcover, 172 pages, 5" x 7.25" • $18
audio: 2-CD set, read by Jon Schreiber • $20

The Four Relationships *and Other Essential Insights*

– by Jon Schreiber

The Four Relationships—our relationship to the body, our relationship to the outside world, our relationship to ourself, and our relationship to our True nature—provide a universal framework that enables us to usefully relate to the ingredients and issues of our life, and to find a meaningful posture and approach to the questions life places in front of us. This book explores the principles and philosophy of Breema.

available in print, audio, and eBook format
print: hardcover, 160 pages, 5" x 7.25" • $18
audio: 2-CD set, read by Jon Schreiber • $20

Waking Up to This Moment:
The Essential Meaning of Breema

– by Jon Schreiber

To the extent you are available at this moment, you are doing Breema. It's as simple as that. If you keep this direction clear for yourself and always work with it, you can come to a taste—the taste of being present. Instead of being drawn to the past or future, where you have been conditioned to live, it's possible to live your life with meaning and purpose in the present.

available in print & audio
print: hardcover, 168 pages, 7" x 9"
          60 color photos • $25
audio: 2-CD set, read by Jon Schreiber • $20

Child of Existence, Child of Society – by Jon Schreiber

There are two parts of us—the child of Existence and the child of society. The child of society is our acquired aspect, acquired from our education, from books, movies, radio, television, newspapers, the Internet. But we're more than that. We have also been given something by Existence. The child of Existence is our essential aspect, what we are in reality. The aim is to move from this outer part, this acquired part, towards the inner part—to find this essential part of ourself.

available in print & audio
print: hardcover, 208 pages, 5" x 7.25" • $18
audio: 2-CD set, read by Jon Schreiber • $20

Your Home Is the Entire Cosmos: *The Wisdom of Breema*

– by Jon Schreiber

The desire to know, to be, and to understand is the essential heritage of being human. The most meaningful aspect of that desire is the desire to know oneself, to be oneself, and to understand oneself. Even though we don't know what "self" means, this gives us direction. It points towards *you*. In order to develop, you need to know yourself. To the extent you know yourself, you know other things, too.

print: hardcover, 192 pages, 5" x 7.25" • $18 ·

In the Heart of the Moment: *Essential Poetry*

– collected by Jon Schreiber

These poems are doorways that open into the heart of Breema as a teaching for Self-understanding, and for understanding the world and our place and purpose in it.

print: hardcover, 112 pages, 5.25" x 8" • $15

In the Garden of All Possibilities: *Essential Poetry*

– collected by Jon Schreiber

These poems are meant to harmonize our inner aspect and bring it into equilibrium with Existence. Their vibration and sequence create a meaning. When you listen, you become an instrument. The poems tune you, and you resonate with their music.

print: hardcover, 112 pages, 5.25" x 8" • $15

The Taste of Being Present: *Essential Wisdom of Breema*

– by Jon Schreiber

You have to know where you are, wherever you are. Establish one "marker"—I am here in this moment. This first step is the most important thing in the world! Wherever you are, be where you are. Then, you can see the next step.

You study Breema in order to study yourself. You do Breema in order to be yourself. Being yourself means body, mind, and feelings functioning in the receptive state, receiving Conscious energy from your True nature. In those moments, you know yourself.

available in print & audio
print: hardcover, 172 pages, 5" x 7.25" • $18
audio: 2-CD set, read by Jon Schreiber • $20

Real Health Means Harmony with Existence:
The Art of Practicing Breema – by Jon Schreiber

You do Breema in order to become present, and by remaining present, to have presence, which is to receive the emanation of what *is*. In that, your *Being* participates. Understanding is a property of Being, and Being is in harmony with what is.

print: hardcover, 208 pages, 5" x 7.25" • $18

First You Have to *Be*:
The Nine Principles of Harmony in Breema and Life

– by Jon Schreiber

The purpose of Breema bodywork, Self-Breema exercises, and Breema's philosophy is to show us a new way of life—the way to be yourself in life, the way to participate in life, not in the reactive state, but in the active state, with body and mind together. From there, you have a chance to come to the receptive state—body, mind, and feelings together.

available in print & audio
print: hardcover, 192 pages, 5" x 7.25" • $18
audio: 2-CD set, read by Jon Schreiber • $20

Coming to Yourself: *The Art of Practicing Breema*

– by Jon Schreiber

To see things as they are, we have to *be* as we are. The taste of Being is received in the absence of thoughts, feelings, and sensations. When we receive that taste, we can see thoughts as thoughts, feelings as feelings, sensations as sensations. By not identifying with them, we enter into the awareness of our existence.

print: hardcover, 208 pages, 5" x 7.25" • $19

Seeing Things As They Really Are

– by Jon Schreiber

You can only see things as they really are when you see yourself as you are in relation to them. It means to see things as a part of your existence, not as separate phenomena. Existence is one unified whole—nothing separate exists. There is one life force, and it enters into everything that has been created. That means it also flows through you. When you are present, you experience it.

print: hardcover, 192 pages, 5" x 7.25" • $19

Call **510.428.0937** to order **Breema Center books & CDs,**
or see our Bookstore at: **breema.com**
Check your favorite online stores for our eBooks.